BOOKS BY MARIE PONSOT

THE BIRD CATCHER   1998

THE GREEN DARK   1988

ADMIT IMPEDIMENT   1981

TRUE MINDS   1957

THE BIRD CATCHER

THE
BIRD
CATCHER

POEMS BY

MARIE PONSOT

ALFRED A. KNOPF

NEW YORK

1998

THIS IS A BORZOI BOOK
PUBLISHED BY ALFRED A. KNOPF, INC.

www.randomhouse.com

Some of the poems in this volume were originally published in periodicals, as follows:

COMMONWEAL: Better; Even (1); Explorers Cry Out Unheard; Oceans; One Is One; Persephone Packing; The Title's Last; Unplugged

KENYON REVIEW: All Wet; Around a Beautiful Theory; Ghazals for Djuna Barnes: the Fall Back; Pourriture Noble

THE NEW YORKER: Even (III)

PARIS REVIEW: For My Old Self, at Notre Dame; Even (IV)

SOUTHWEST REVIEW: Separate; In the Swim

WESTERN HUMANITIES: Old Mama Saturday

Two Acknowledgments:

The form used in the poems "Living Room" and "Roundstone Cove" is the useful invention of the eminent Americanist Bette Weidman; it is a tritina.

The form used in "Movers and Shakers," "All Wet," and "Snap Shots" I learned in a party game in Beijing, where each stanza was composed by a different poet. In my three poems each stanza was written by me but at different times, a day or a month apart. My host in Beijing called the form "dragons running."

Library of Congress Cataloging-in-Publication Data

Ponsot, Marie.
    The bird catcher : poems / by Marie Ponsot.
      p. cm.
    ISBN 0-375-40135-0
    I. Title.
PS3531.O4985 1998   97-50402
811'.54—dc21   CIP

Manufactured in the United States of America
First Edition

CONTENTS

To the Muse of Doorways Edges Verges   3

I *FOR MY OLD SELF*

"I've Been Around: It Gets Me Nowhere."   7
Restoring My House   9
"Trois Petits Tours et Puis . . ."   11
Old Mama Saturday   12
Northampton Style   13
Incomparable Assumptions   14
The Title's Last   16
Gradual   17
One Is One   18
Pourriture Noble   19
For My Old Self, At Notre-Dame   21

II *SEPARATE, IN THE SWIM*

The Border   25
Separate, In the Swim   27
The Story After the Story   29
Living Room   31
After the Pastoral   32
Autumn Clean-up   33
Roundstone Cove   34
Non-Vegetarian   35
Unplugged   36
Better   37
Reminder   38
We Are Imagined   39

III *THE SPLIT IMAGE OF ATTENTION*

The Split Image of Attention   43
Reading a Large Serving Dish   44
Skimming Raw Folk Material   45
Analysis   46
Birthday   47
Endoxa, or, Reputable Opinions   49
Around a Beautiful Theory   50
Two Questions   54
A Determined Present   57
Movers and Shakers   58
In Favor of Good Dreams   59
Pre-Text   60
For Djuna Barnes as Julie Ryder   61
Taking Thought   62

IV *EXPLORERS CRY OUT UNHEARD*

Explorers Cry Out Unheard   65
Winter   66
All Wet   67
Snap Shots   69
Underbutter   71
Persephone, Packing   72
Festival of Bread   74
Full Moon, Unstressed Measures   75
Oceans   78
Foreign Correspondent   79
Against the Dark, New Poets Rise   81
What the Worn Rhymes Found   82
Climbing in Big Bend National Park   83
Even   84

THE BIRD CATCHER

TO THE MUSE OF DOORWAYS EDGES VERGES

Tall in the doorway stands
the gentle visitor.
I catch my breath

      (She's quite deaf,
      not interested in
      details of my decor.
      Her few words amaze me.
      Her visits are irregular,
      brief. When our eyes meet,
      how I am drawn to her.
      I keep honey cakes, in case,
      in the freezer. Once
      she stayed for tea.)

She smiles. She speaks up, some.
Each word ravishes,
bright with the sciences
she practices
in the music business.

"One day, when you're not dumb,
you must come
to my place," she says,
and vanishes.

I   *For My Old Self*

"I'VE BEEN AROUND: IT GETS ME NOWHERE."

"Cuncta fui; conducit nihil." V. Aurelius

I am the woman always too young to be
holding the diamond the baby exulting.

I am the worker afraid of the rules & the boss; my
salary heats the house where I feed many children.

I am packing my bags for coming & going
& going much further than ever before.

> Though elsewhere gets me nowhere
> place is not a problem.
> Feet keep me going,
> the impressive exporters
> of what place is about. Maps—
> gold on parchment or printed
> Mobil travel ads—lay it all out.
>
> But over every place, time goes
> remote, a cloud-cover question.
> You, in love with your castle, your jet,
> your well-invested dollars
> and I with my moving
> dictionaries & binoculars
> are both almost out of it,
> too far gone to find a bin
> with stores of more time in.
> A decade, a week, a second, then
> time shrugs and shudders out of touch
> into a perfect fit,
> and that's it.

I am the dog I let out in the morning
wagging & panting at the open door.

I am the foresworn child in the swing
arching & pumping, practicing, "More, more!"

I'm the crossword puzzle time & place
bound at the end by their loose embrace.

RESTORING MY HOUSE

Her husband dead, my grandmother destroyed
every photo of herself. I helped find them,
did as she asked, and didn't tell.
"Paper ghosts," she said, "that's all they are."

Now I undo my packages long in storage.
Crowded in notebooks or folders,
stapled or separated anyhow,
scrawled or machine-stricken,
these are words someone had, some I
had to say, green or seasoned, for myself.

My hands feel dull. Paper-coating
nasties the pores shut. Dusty in windowlight,
some edges still cut mean. Crumpled, some chip.

I rise from the mess on the living-room floor,
yank the stuck flue open, match the first lot
to their fire-life
transparent in its speech.
It murmurs over them. Lullaby
of the unknown life-giver, faceless,
earlier even than Hertha,
the hearth's the oldest deity
and my good riddance.

Longing to clear out
the debris of keeping, I feed in
records of years I need no record of.
They have gone dry at last.

They catch and blaze. I hook out
the backlog, oak seasoned for welcome.
Already a little charred,
it begins to burn.

Nodes of sunspurt interrupt then spread the fire.
Its burning gestures are harmonious.
At each downfall compensation flares
in a quick tree of flame.

The leaves I have torn up
turn into the hum of a
budding comfort disclosing
along a tree of transforming.

This task is in praise of ancestors,
those still working fireplaces
to whom I come when the next task

is to get out from under, hungry
to open up images
into the presence of absence
of images, and change.

"TROIS PETITS TOURS ET PUIS . . ."

She gives him paper and a fine-nibbed pen;
he discovers the world and makes a map.
She gives him boots and a Havaheart trap,
Peterson guides, tent, backpack, fish-hooks, then
rehearses the uses of the North Star.

He leaves a trail of breadcrumbs down the road.
He mails back snapshots of himself & his load
borne almost a mile till he thumbed a car
& hitched to where he spread his picnic out.
His assets (food & use of gear) he lends
to the driver. He learns he likes to play fair.
That all this must please her he does not doubt.

His map omits her. His snapshots go to friends.
A fresh music fills her house, a fresh air.

OLD MAMA SATURDAY

("Saturday's Child Must Work for a Living.")

"I'm moving from Grief Street.
Taxes are high here
though the mortgage's cheap.

The house is well built.
With stuff to protect, that
mattered to me,
the security.

These things that I mind,
you know, aren't mine.
I mind minding them.
They weigh on my mind.

I don't mind them well.
I haven't got the knack
of kindly minding.
I say Take them back
but you never do.

When I throw them out
it may frighten you
and maybe me too.

      Maybe
it will empty me
too emptily

and keep me here
asleep, at sea
under the guilt quilt,
under the you tree."

NORTHAMPTON STYLE

Evening falls. Someone's playing a dulcimer
Northampton-style, on the porch out back.
Its voice touches and parts the air of summer,

as if it swam to time us down a river
where we dive and leave a single track
as evening falls. Someone's playing a dulcimer

that lets us wash our mix of dreams together.
Delicate, tacit, we engage in our act;
its voice touches and parts the air of summer.

When we disentangle you are not with her
I am not with him. Redress calls for tact.
Evening falls. Someone's playing a dulcimer

still. A small breeze rises and the leaves stir
as uneasy as we, while the woods go black;
its voice touches and parts the air of summer

and lets darkness enter us; our strings go slack
though the player keeps up his plangent attack.
Evening falls. Someone's playing a dulcimer;
its voice touches and parts the air of summer.

INCOMPARABLE ASSUMPTIONS

The lilium (rubrum, tall,
leaves spiralled up its spike)
spreads like Siva elegant arms,
many of them.

To perform its counterbalancing
each arm is weighted at the end
with long buds, daily
thicker heavier.

Stemmed above them, terminal,
one bud's flying open, fragrant.
Its back-bending petals blush,
full of grace, for today.
(Today's the awkward August
Feast, August Assumption;
rubrum blooms late for a lily.)

For two months leaf-hoppers beetles
slugs have tried it but no luck.
Out from its stake it lurches
into direct sun to suck up more
("More!") light, shading the dahlias.
It does well here
free though staked firm,
delivered from evil by
the nature of rubrum, unable
to go wrong or to do right or
guess at good or evil done to it—
an innocence only natural.

It gives the gardener
unremarked behind such blossoming
a measure:
            of the action & flavor
innocence would assume for her
(a habit of vigorous growth
throughout her!) if she
were vegetal and innocent.

THE TITLE'S LAST

Here's the best joke, though its flavor is salt:
the bad company I've kept, the bad risks I've run
have left me standing (a figure of fun
but) one at whose shadow some strangers halt.

I've been pole when some asked, so they could vault
supported, high as they like, letting me drop
intact, and roll safe to a grassy stop.
We've gone our ways with pleasure and without fault,
they to the next race, I to the next use
poles are put to by the great competitors.

Self-schooled I've been fish, ocean floors
wrinkling my shadow, flashing free, loose,
in my long survival of all I've done—
for sharks that bite me eat death by poison,
le requin qui me mord s'empoisonne.

GRADUAL

(on September 14, Feast of the Exaltation)

This serene and mortal afternoon
slides the late summer
down a course of outwardness.
I take it in.

Now & then soft gusts stir the air.
Between them sun fills the stillness, windless.
White pinetrees filter the sun rays.
Their needles glisten; the light's increased.

Jays on look-out shriek: Enemies!
Watch your back! The non-human cries
pluck me out of the hush I hide grief in.
Pain I've kept hoarded flares up & off.
It gets smaller. It goes on out
to roost with the jays, simmering down
under treecrowns invisible from here.

Slowly westering, full
light slips invisibly
toward slant.

Collected clouds thin out flat,
their gradual ribboning
just visibly eastering.

ONE IS ONE

Heart, you bully, you punk, I'm wrecked, I'm shocked
stiff. You? you still try to rule the world—though
I've got you: identified, starving, locked
in a cage you will not leave alive, no
matter how you hate it, pound its walls,
& thrill its corridors with messages.

Brute. Spy. I trusted you. Now you reel & brawl
in your cell but I'm deaf to your rages,
your greed to go solo, your eloquent
threats of worse things you (knowing me) could do.
You scare me, bragging you're a double agent

since jailers are prisoners' prisoners too.
Think! Reform! Make us one. Join the rest of us,
and joy may come, and make its test of us.

POURRITURE NOBLE

a moral tale, for Sauternes, the fungus cenaria, *and the wild old*

Never prophesy.
You can't. So don't try.
Lust, pride, and lethargy
may cause us misery
or bliss.
The meanest mistake
has a point to make.
Hear this—
what his vintner d'Eyquem said
once the lord d'Eyquem was dead:
  "The wine that year promised bad or none.
  He'd let it go too late.
  Rot had crawled through all the vines,
  greasy scum on every cluster
  dangling at the crotches of the leaves.
  Should have been long picked
  but he'd said, 'No. Wait for me,'
  off to wait on a new woman,
  grapes on the verge of ripe
  when he left. Coupling kept him
  till rot wrapped the grapes like lace
  & by the time she'd kicked him out
  the sun had got them, they hung
  shriveled in the blast.

  Well, he rode home cocky
  & bullied the grapes into the vats
  rot & all, spoiled grapes, too old,
  too soon squeezed dry.
       The wine makes.
  The wine makes thick, gold-colored,

& pours like honey.
We try it. Fantastic!
not like honey, punchy,
you've never drunk anything like it—
refreshing, in a rush
over a heat that slows your throat—
wanting to keep that flavor
stuck to the edge of your tongue
where your taste is, keep it
like the best bouquet you can remember
of sundown summer & someone coming
to you smiling. The taste has odor
like a new country, so fine
at first you can't take it in
it's so strange. It's beautiful
& believe me you love to go slow."

moral:

Age is not
all dry rot.
It's never too late.
Sweet is your real estate.

FOR MY OLD SELF, AT NOTRE-DAME:
fluctuat nec mergitur

The dark madonna cut from a knot of wood
has robes whose folds make waves against the grain
and a touching face—noble in side view,
impish or childish seen head-on from above.
The wood has the rich stain of tannin, raised
to all-color lustre by the steep of time.

The mouths of her shadows are pursed by time
to suck sun-lit memories from the wood.
Freezing damp and candle-smut have raised
her eyebrows into wings flung up by the grain,
caught in the light of bulbs plugged high above.
She stands alert, as if hailed, with beasts in view.

Outside on the jeweled river-ship, I view
a girl's back, walking off. Oh. Just in time
I shut up. She'd never hear me shout above
the tour-guides and ski-skate kids. How I would
have liked to see her face again, the grain
of beauty on her forehead, her chin raised

startled; her Who are you? wild, a question raised
by seeing me, an old woman, in plain view.
Time is a tree in me; in her it's a grain
ready to plant. I go back in, taking my time
leafy among stone trunks that soar in stone woods
where incense drifts, misty, lit pink from above.

She's headed for her hotel room then above
Cluny's garden. She'll sit there then, feet raised,
notebook on her knees, to write. Maybe she would
have heard, turned, known us both in a larger view
and caught my age in the freshness of its time.
She dreads clocks, she says. Such dry rot warps the grain.

They still say mass here. Wine and wheat-grain
digest to flesh in words that float above
six kneeling women, a man dressed outside time,
and the dark madonna, her baby raised
dangerously high to pull in our view.
Magic dame, cut knot, your ancient wood

would reach back to teach her if it could. Spring rain.
Through it I call to thank her, loud above
the joy she raised me for, this softfall. Sweet time.

I I   *Separate, In the Swim*

THE BORDER
(Annuals & Perennials, Mixed)

She kneels to the yellow short flowers
velvety, feathery, lit. Pansies
are for thoughts, she knows,
and, Pick lots but pick them
in the morning so they last.

The can of salted water is for slugs.
It kills them dead, quietly.
She finds one bigger than her thumb.
She looks away to drop it in but
hears it drop. She's taller this year;
standing she can gaze downward into
the iris Queen Maud a white crown
on the stem that presents it
above the crowded pansy border.

Next Saturday at Dorothea's wedding
she'll be the flower girl
with a crown of baby's breath clipped
to her slippery dutch-bob hair.

She must remember / she'd better practice
Left Foot First, this week,
every time she walks.
Grandma says, It's all right, dear,
all eyes will be on the bride.

The earliest tree peony is out,
alba, it smells like roses among
the garden's almost-summer smell.

She sits on the steps; they're hot
not too hot. She picks up her blue pipe.
Beside her the bowl
holds water gluey with soap
& drops of grandma's glycerine.
The pipe-cup breaks its disk of light.

Trying to be even & be slow
she bites on the pipe-stem.
Her breath steadies;
she blows out a bubble,
another, the two
float over the pansies
into the bridal-wreath bush
and disappear.

Getting married is like that.
Getting married is not like that.

SEPARATE, IN THE SWIM
(Temara Plage, Morocco)

Oiled and drowsy, idling in a sling
of turquoise cotton, you take the sun.

I stow my rings, cash, shirt, & frayed
cords of connection under your chair.

I cross bands of hot sand then damp cool,
to the waves rustling up
broken by the aim of wave, the idea
that picks up the water
and throws it at the shore.

Invading the invading sea, leaning to it
arms at an angle, I wade in slowly,
weight forward, leading with my knees,
soft-jumping in answer to wave-swell.

Wet to the hips I dive under
and swim turning in to pleasure.
The sea surges inshore. I surge out.

The seas alter me and alter after me,
allowing me a horizontal stride.
Armstrokes & legstrokes echo in my cells
heating the circuit of blood.

Each stroke starts a far drumming
clumping the kelp, helping
shells and rubbish decay into sand.
I press out a pulse (it will

throb back as another pulse) along
the sea-floor and the furthest beaches.
In this stretch of the Atlantic
the whole Atlantic operates.

As I ride, its broad cast evokes
my tiny unity, a pod, a person.

Thanks to the closure of skin
I'm forking the tune I'm part of
though my part is played moving
on a different instrument.
I hear the converse of wave-work
fluid in counterpoint, the current
unrupturing. I push: the Atlantic
resists so that I can push myself

toward a music which on this scale
is balance, balancing buoyancies,
able to condense me back out with it
having carried my will
forward a while before
it carries me to shore.

You have slept.
You have taken the sun.
I towel myself dry.

THE STORY AFTER THE STORY

In bubbles to the elbow, on my knees,
I am washing children. You are laughing,
pleased to observe me at my mysteries.

Antoine & Will giggle as I sluice their backs.
My knees soaked by local tidal splashes
creak as I stand and towel two relaxed

bed-ready boys. I crib them, warm in their
soft shirts, & sit to eat a bruised sweet apple
as I nurse Chris and float on mild air

a story for everyone; Monique & Denis
settle on child-chairs; we are a tangle,
bitch and pups, in the oldest comity.

You like that less, leave us for the kitchen
to finish the fruit and cheese. The ample
story falls short on me. My mind itches.

Sighing & smiling Antoine drops to sleep.
Will lies awake, only his eyes active.
Monique trusts the story somehow to keep

mapping new ways home through more & more world.
Chris drowses. Will's eyelids lift up, lapse back.
Denis' fists lie in his lap, loosely curled.

I am willing them one by one to sleep.
The story wanders in its adjectives.
Chris' mouth clamps down, lets go, breathes deep.

Humming & murmuring I bed them all.
Monique tells a soft story, managing
me into mind with her as she too falls.

I rise in joy, ready, the child-work done.
I find you have gone out. A radical
of loss cancels what we might have become.

LIVING ROOM

The window's old & paint-stuck in its frame.
If we force it open the glass may break.
Broken windows cut, and let in the cold

to sharpen house-warm air with outside cold
that aches to buckle every saving frame
& let the wind drive ice in through the break

till chair cupboard walls stormhit all goods break.
The family picture, wrecked, soaked in cold,
would slip wet & dangling out of its frame.

Framed, it's a wind-break. It averts the worst cold.

AFTER THE PASTORAL

Just after dusk the tulips still show yellow.

This year my child goes where I can't follow.
My first is gone, the one where I began.
"Come back," I whisper. "Come in if you can."
Silence I step out, ferocious with fear.
Dread enters my one, trance my other, ear.
The tulips fade. I drowse until dawn breaks.
My eyes open. I force myself awake.
Cowbirds crowd the ground wherever I look.

Where soft mouths taste the night, it sets its hook.

AUTUMN CLEAN-UP

There she is in her garden
bowing & dipping, reaching
stretched with her shears—
a Ceres commanding forces
no one else any more fears.

The garden's not enclosed.
It encloses her. It helps her
hold her joy. (She is
too shy for transports.)

It helps keep her whole
when grief for unchangeable reasons
waits to gnaw a tunnel in her
to run around wild in,
grinding its little teeth,
eager to begin.

ROUNDSTONE COVE

The wind rises. The sea snarls in the fog
far from the attentive beaches of childhood—
no picnic, no striped chairs, no sand, no sun.

Here even by day cliffs obstruct the sun;
moonlight miles out mocks this abyss of fog.
I walk big-bellied, lost in motherhood,

hunched in a shell of coat, a blindered hood.
Alone a long time, I remember sun—
poor magic effort to undo the fog.

Fog hoods me. But the hood of fog is sun.

NON-VEGETARIAN

It haunts us, the misappropriated flesh,
be it Pelops' shoulder after Demeter's feast
or Adam's rib supporting Eve's new breasts,
or the nameless root of Gilgamesh.

Who am I that a given beast must die
to stake the smoulder of my blood or eyes?
Were only milk, fruit, honey to supply
my table, I would not starve but thrive.

But then the richer goods I misappropriate
(time wasted, help withheld, mean words for great)
would blaze forth and nag me to repudiate
the habitual greed of my normal state.

My guts delight twice in the death I dine on,
once for hunger, once for what meat distracts me from.

UNPLUGGED

Once, you were translucent; you stood between
me and the source; you tempered the light, became
the light I chose to see by. I have seen
by earth-light, straight, for a long time now. I name
the objects, powerful, that I have kept:
my bed, my laundry, my pantry, my stairs.

You took the valuables when you left.
Abandoning our old lamps and chairs
you unscrewed that incandescent choice of mine:
you my constant, the light-speed I saw by.
Disconnected you vanished. I define
growing things one by one, with my own eyes.

I miss, dismiss the lust for free obedience.
In natural light the world is immense.

BETTER

After a long wet season the rain's let up.
The list my life was on was critical;
reproach soaked it and infected my ears.
I hid, deaf and blind, my skin my hospital,
in the inoperable ache of fear.

Today the rain stops. I can hear! Trees drip.
They spatter & whisper as I walk their
breathing avenue. The wind has died back;
edge-catching light elaborates the air.

From the road car-tunes rush close then slacken.
I climb the green hill. There at last I reach
a figured stillness where no nightmares slide.

Green leaves turn inside out to grow. They breach
their barriers. I come, eyes wide, outside.

REMINDER

I am rich I am poor. Time is all I own.
I spend or hoard it for experience.
By the bitten wound the biting tooth is known.

Thrift is a venomous error, then, a stone
named bread or cash to support the pretense
that I'm rich. I am poor; time is all I own . . .

though I hold to memory: how spent time shone
as you approached, and the light loomed immense.
By the bitten wound the biting tooth is known,

though scars fade. I have memory on loan
while it evaporates; though it be dense
& I am rich, I am poor. Time is all I own

to sustain me—the moonlit skeleton
that holds my whole life in moving suspense.
By the bitten wound the biting tooth is known.

Ownership's brief, random, a suite of events.
If the past is long the future's short. Since
I am rich I am poor. Time is all I own.
By the bitten wound the biting tooth is known.

WE ARE IMAGINED

Time has expanded between us, like the spread
stain of a war we weren't fighting in.
Neutrals shed history. We have shed
the gentle sense we made together then.

      I suppose routs of soldiers have occupied
      the house we left unplanned-for—
      raw troops, more tired than terrified.
      Their shit and cook-fires star the floor.
      Our garden's gone to seed. Our valuables
      we left locked in a bomb-cellar at the foreign
      bank. We, who are now one and one and never
      there, will never see it again.

      I suppose one night a soldier
      finds by flashlight the necklace
      you gave me. He pockets the blue stones
      to send to his girl back home
      well out of the war zone.
      He wonders whose it once was.
      He guesses, that is, at us two.

      I suppose his idea imagines
      that the war will end & we
      will mourn the necklace missing it
      while he'll smile at his bride
      rounding to pregnancy,
      the beads' blue-violet shadow
      above her cotton summer dress;

and he will caress her arm & tell
about the war including
the worst of it, & confess,
and she will cry for him
but not make a fuss.

And they will chat & imagine
something compensatory
happening for us.

III *The Split Image of Attention*

THE SPLIT IMAGE OF ATTENTION
(illuminated MS, Trinity College, Dublin)

Saints in the *Book of Dimma*
deserve their double-rainbow eyes
for seeing form & structure,
skin & skeleton, both
at once. Great
lovers of instruction,
mouths empty, they tip
their earlobes forward
the better to lock in
the learning
inviting it as it enters and is intimate
with their diamond-cut holy
double-bolted ears.

I look to the next page where
having taken as their text
a wordshape so precipitous
it makes crystals of their tears

they divine the structuring
nature of genesis

& their eyes irradiate
on their own   full
of fear   hearing the meaning
of shooting stars.

READING A LARGE SERVING DISH
(Greek, ca. 400 BC, Chicago Art Institute)

Persephone white-faced
carries her vegetal cross
on a stalk perpendicular
over her shoulder as she heads
up & out for home
& mother, her brilliant mother.

Closing, Hell's house lies behind her
(and, of course, opening, before).

Four creamy horses
implacably processional
are hauling her chariot
—red-orange on black ceramic—
toward her spring turn of sky.
They head for the edge
of the dish of plenty that honors
her style of exchange (exile for exile)
and her game of rounders (no winners, no losers)
her poverty her plenty.

> The dish itself is Demosthenes' age.
> Its suave lines issue its invitation,
> open-ended, a strange attractor.

> It tells you it will
> if you eat from it teach
> your deepening night to brighten
> at the depth where no gesture
> is straightforward or false,
> and you do not need to expect
> you can rise beyond suffering.

SKIMMING RAW FOLK MATERIAL

The tale has bends in it. What can it mean
that he leaves on a quest for a talking horse

but comes back with a princess? In between
she gives him falcon-power, but remorse
starves him since he won't kill small game. (He'd feast
if the hut on chicken-legs hopped a snow-hid course
twirling before him through the woods.) He runs east,
west, sleep deprived till he finds the last word
for sleep, but forgets it when a wakeful beast
proves to him his mother tongue's absurd.

It's about what all stories are about,
the bargain they offer or deny the heart:
to get home, leave home; pack; at dawn set out
on a trip dusk closes where it started.

ANALYSIS

Analysis prefers a mountain lake
without tributaries to account for.
It can't stand random splashing, can't just take
its clothes off and jump in. Its designs score
by degrees: first it looks, till it seizes
a sense of the whole; then it stares some more,
till the rippling surface stills & freezes.
Its bubbles flatten hard and rim the shore.

And now analysis cuts the ice to bits,
tens or thousands, each a telling device
flashing "lake" in part-song, true in how it fits
the cutter's visionary set for ice.

Patterns lapse in a bliss of signal mist
which concludes in the swim of the analyst.

BIRTHDAY
(for Rosemary Deen)

In for the winter, your Christmas Cactus
shouts "Rose" & shoots its flame-sleek flowers out
in doubles at the end of each dark stem.
I can't copy such plenty. But I can
proclaim how well its structure celebrates
the lived poetic all your born days state.

When in thin winter you let summer state
its essential green by heating for us
jars of basil couched in oil, we celebrate
earth work sun work your work, opened out
when we most want freshness, in rites which can
retrace the tides of summer time must stem.

Autumn is inward. Wild buds sleep in stem,
rapt secret in their generative state.
November sends you in, with all you can
hold of harvest. Fruits you serve to us
you save in seed, too, then sort the seeds out.
Identified, they concelebrate.

That analysis is ours to celebrate.
Grain by grain you loft seeds into system
as in sonnets the ripe-dropped thought springs out.
Labeled, seeds shape the form their nature states.
You, general & scrupulous,
recast the particulars until we scan

the song-score of the year, because you can.
Gourds to seeds, words to poems celebrate
new places you flag as common to us,
their nature prized by so apt a system
we enter it like a long-lost mental state,
and dump our own sacks of odd fact-bits out.

We count on you. Laughing, you'll figure them out.
Elements, caught quick—as you always can—
flash-melt old grids down to a fluid state.
Fact-bits, basil, cactus, we, concelebrate
change as the blossoming source of system.
We breathe the green we eat. Time swims in us.

You flower for us flaring out from a stem
whose perennial seed-reach can make fall state
the final primal cause you celebrate.

ENDOXA, OR, REPUTABLE OPINIONS
(Aristotle, Bahktin, T. Berry)

The tailor's sophist power grows
till young philosophy speaks, and shows
the emperor has no clothes.

Dialectic's spiral spins
beyond mere opinion, to propose:
the emperor's skin
is the emperor's clothes,
the dress the emperor's always in.

Boy Aristotle mapped these minds:
"What philosophy knows
and dialectic probes,
no sophist can find."

I unlike Aristotle watch
the world I reach disclose
what dialectic misses:

where I live is shiftier
than that fictive emperor is.

There is no cosmos,
just a cosmogenesis.

AROUND A BEAUTIFUL THEORY
(at the Getty Museum, Santa Monica)

I

Answering warriors
the washerwoman at the river, glancing
down the morning current
toward a bloody afternoon, said,
"I see red. I see red. I see red."

death sentences
instances of truth

& here in the hurt world
whose denials root in the soil
of the fear of dying,
the True rushed back to me from exile:
        Blood lends us a life-line.
        Death ends that lending.
        We shall die. We can say that's true.

But wait! to leap
(like a new hermeneutic
with antic old tricks)
from True to Beautiful
can't be done. It's
too dull, idle,
irresponsible, and unpopular.

II

Last week in Santa Monica
I almost got a grip on it.
If I'd been credentialled & dressed right,
an attentive Getty curator
might have let me hold
    for a minute
    round in the round of my palm
out of its lit niche
the rock crystal figure
whose attributes are love
(Aphrodite Artemis Is/
is) rising from trans
parent seas, her antecedents
undefined primitives
doubtful of access

    yet she always is always the one
    in whose hand we are already held: love.

III

It's only an artifact. It only looks
lit from within.
I'd have given her right back.

The hand is blind.

It's OK that the hand is blind.
Weight's what my hand wants,
the rosy body readable,
its density held to be brilliant,
its language of feeling
tactile, not a crack in it.

Erasing miss-pelt joylessness
it writes the text of the beautiful
    love we subscribe to
    when accurately read.

Let it speak, and it speaks
an embodying beauty
so quick it can re-mind
the loved dead (their everydays dead)
as they (their beauty resisting
obliteration) are smuggled back in
through the vent the little beauty opens
to air the beautiful they were for us.
Re-membered, their presence gleams,
their absence unaccounted for here,

where fear of the beautiful
roots under the roots of fear.

Uninstructed, empty-handed, I can't
account for the commonly beautiful
    gardener washing the lettuces
    busdriver close-shaving corners
    teenager waiting on tables
or the para site panache of any joy

        IV

but look, I hold them harmless
in the turnkey question of the gap
the statue makes. Unearthed
she is giving herself airs,
ordering, "Use your eyes.
See. See. See."

Quiet, on her bright shelf, laid bare
she comes as love's summoner
tumbling in the lump of quartz.
The very track-light is beautiful.
Alive in it, curator,
I give myself airs

TWO QUESTIONS

*(for E. Coleman, L. Ferlinghetti, E. Fontinell, G. Mally, D. Yezzo,
all men of good will and sometime armed forces)*

I

Dropped
brilliant
in such windrush he
can't scream
he's moving too
fast in the pitchblack
falling his
parachute hot buckles & charred string

he is on fire he hits salt
water, goes out   as he
goes under. It chokes with
him in his throat,
that shout.

Fire, the flare human, the
body of burning plunging,
shot star sea-quenched:
   .. fifty years on fire in my mind.

Second hand. Dreamed, dreamed,
a silence of scream, heat
into cold, extinguishing.
Waked by, wept for, guessed at,
an ignorant dream, dreaming those
who flew to kill again toward gunfire
flew killed flew killed flew   But he

burned, that boy, my age, Lt. Little,
prayed for in my parish monthly thirty years
till his mother died; who else would remember?
His lovers at then twenty-one
have long loved others. Only those
who made him up out of anguish
ignorant among war news remember
what the order of murder made.

II

Wasp & osprey flee our ring of discord
but now & then—as if some beast were fat
& we winter-struck with hunger—
we close in on it flourishing weaponry
and war makes meat of some.

In their poor young butchers
otherwise virtuous   it taints memory
with ownerless bitterness.

Our catch-basin cities swirl with blood
until—some larder stocked—we stop
come home   wash up   and restore
peace as if there were no war.

If slaughter always alters our memory
if brutal mistakes are fatal so far

& if I—no Amazon, no Lysistrata—agree
no life is free of brute fatality

what is a safe childhood for?

of what is war the history?

A DETERMINED PRESENT

Chance as it maps
the next necessity
steps her, step by step,
as if she is free.

Often enough, she finds herself
where she never chose to be:
in winter, under the prickly
branches of a Christmas tree;
or, come summer, thirsty
far from the general store
at a picnic table in New Hampshire
outside the local mental hospital
named Gethsemane, originally.

MOVERS AND SHAKERS

The Round Barn vaults a floor blessed
by the prayers of feet, a music threshed
by steppers ascending into long forgetfulness.

When winter lasts too long the prisoner
is tempted to become her own cage.

Though it dine on its own self,
for a tadpole
frog is heaven.

The architect of frog is damsel-fly,
a mortal/vital alchemy.

Vein and artery vital and inimical
collaborate in capillaries—
take exchange, give thanks.

Independent (in that best dream) all take
their time, to enjoy each other's company.

Summer caucasians tan and enjoy
a bronzed indifference, pretending
it eases the longing for equality.

Ice since autumn, sun eases its edges and
the brook starts a spring conversation.

IN FAVOR OF GOOD DREAMS
(a rann)

Memory,
hum wordless images, be
tuneful color for these dreams
whose greywashed streams greywash me.

In sleep-sprawl
my rare knives are hospital
not sexual; what they cut's
not mythic but surgical

error out,
banning the disease of doubt,
forcing steely discipline
to thin-slit my skin without

cruelty
or joy; knives act craftily
in inert flesh gone dumb.
But lovers come clumsily,

carefully,
carelessly, most patiently
together. Seek for me those
uncut roses, memory.

PRE-TEXT
(for Douglas, at one)

Archaic, his gestures
hieratic, just like Caesar or Sappho
or Mary's Jesus or Ann's Mary or Jane
Austen once, or me or your mother's you

the sudden baby surges to his feet
and sways, head forward, chin high,
arms akimbo, hands dangling idle,
elbows up, as if winged.

The features of his face stand out
amazed, all eyes as his aped posture
sustains him aloft
                a step a step a rush
and he walks,

Young Anyone, his lifted point of view
far beyond the calendar.

What time is it? Firm in time
he is out of date—

like a cellarer for altar wines
tasting many summers in one glass,

or like a grandmother
in whose womb her
granddaughter once
slept in egg inside
grandma's unborn daughter's
folded ovaries.

FOR DJUNA BARNES AS JULIE RYDER

Jacobean savage, hurt while she slept,
words hide the healing secret her life kept.

Her first raw love-letters stay housed with her
all her life. They are from her grandmother.

In dream or in terror her father's mother,
cross-dressed as a plump impresario, beams.

A thread trembles. She falls back drugged with sleep.
The spinner backs away to doze, replete.

Where are you?   silence   *I'm leaving*   fear
I'll fall outside the sky   *You can't lose, dear.*

As its skin is stroked the iris opens
to pleasure in whatever weather happens.

Where are you?   Here love here.   Rapt.   *I teach
the body of joy no body may impeach.*

In the same old fear-dream, new breasts cold,
she buds (age 90) in grandma's buttonhole.

Hark to the measurer: "Bad-Good. Once-Now."
Liar! the once she loves her in is now.

Her tongue forks from her gum the last remaining
crumb of burnt-cork mustache. She swallows the grain.

TAKING THOUGHT

"Tom broods," Grandpa said. His genial brother Tom
gave me wooden dolls, sister-brother twins
from Switzerland. He danced like a charm
and could walk on the river from Brooklyn
to Manhattan in ice-stories he told.
He looked bigger when he brooded. His blue stare
took up the whole room and turned it cold
as he sat, not talking, in his leather chair.

Grandma, longing to bring him out of it,
cooked soup, bacon, coffee, for him to smell;
she sat close across from him and talked, as if
she were two people, saying his part as well
(she was famous for help, in the family)
till he smiled. He smiled like a statue set free.

IV *Explorers Cry Out Unheard*

EXPLORERS CRY OUT UNHEARD

What I have in mind is the last wilderness.

I sweat to learn its heights of sun, scrub, ants,
its gashes full of shadows and odd plants,
as inch by inch it yields to my hard press.

And the way behind me changes as I advance.
If interdependence shapes the biomass,
though I plot my next step by pure chance
I can't go wrong. Even willful deviance
connects me to all the rest. The changing past
includes and can't excerpt me. Memory grants
just the nothing it knows, & my distress
drives me toward the imagined truths I stalk,
those savages. Warned by their haunting talk,
their gestures, I guess they mean no. Or yes.

WINTER

I don't know what to say to you, neighbor,
as you shovel snow from your part of our street
neat in your Greek black. I've waited for
chance to find words; now, by chance, we meet.

We took our boys to the same kindergarten,
thirteen years ago when our husbands went.
Both boys hated school, dropped out feral, dropped in
to separate troubles. You shift snow fast, back bent,
but your boy killed himself, six days dead.

My boy washed your wall when the police were done.
He says, "We weren't friends?" and shakes his head,
"I told him it was great he had that gun,"
and shakes. I shake, close to you, close to you.
You have a path to clear, and so you do.

ALL WET

Underwater, keeled in seas,
zinc the sacrificial anode gives
electrons up to save the sunk hull from salt.

The carving of salt water skirls out beaches
where each wave fall can push softly, a long curve in.

Rain widens the waterfall till the stream
slows, swells, winds up, and topples down
onto lilypads it presses forward on their stems.

Carp drowse among stems sunk in the park lake,
their flesh rich in heavy metals. Eat one and die.

A drip from the tap hits the metal sink
& splats into sunlight, cosmic,
a scatter of smaller drops.

One raindrop on a binocular lens,
and a spectrum haloes the far field.

Haloes dim the form they gild but
by its own edge each object celebrates
the remarkable world.

Personal computers make dry remarks, demanding:
Tea, wine, cups must leave the room.

We're all the wine of something. His Dickens act,
her Wordsworth murmurs, expressed
juices still in ferment when their old children read.

Bones left after dinner simmer down into juices
to make a soup rich as respect or thrift.

As if making allowances
for the non-native limbs of swimmers,
water gives way as I spring into it.

SNAP SHOTS

From the hill road the golf-turf's a postcard
of canny grass. At its hardwood edge
3 deer stall ready to enter or to run.

Curves of clouds run parallel to low earth
where odors flow vertically, circularly.

Echoes of thunder far off flow over fields
& die away under trees that shed
the veiled sound of working leaves.

Late-fall sounds of grass stopping growing
tickle the hearing of ants & crickets.

Insects hear through plaques of listening.
They talk with fictive feet
or sing with greenish wings.

A greens-keeper rides the fairway
back to the first from the eighteenth hole.

West on 18th an old waif
crumples himself throwaway in cardboard.
Pray don't pry. Footstep past.

Night past, the deep-freeze people unbend & stand
to stir the blood puddled in their extremities.

They keep their place
with one shoe on top of their flat cartons
to signify, "Mine, okay?"

Mine says the mole in the parking lot. Mine says the flea on the mole.
Mine says the golfer teeing up. Mine? I say, make mine spring.

UNDERBUTTER

This house has three entrance-ways.
Water flushes its hidden places.

Sun-flush slides rosily off the wall. Dusk dawns.
Cats want out. Deer nose out of the woodlot.
Bats scour the near air as it cools.

Wheel-house: the house rides a cooling land-mass.
Oceans hiding desirable continents
flank it. The round earth turns it as it rides.

Its flank turned to the flank of the hill, the dog
turns off the vista and sniffs at fresh grass.

Angels fly into the fresh vat of cream
& suddenly it's butter.

Sudden awe sudden dread: the visible
fontanelle just under the scalp
of the delicate new-born head.

The delicate tip of the window geranium broke off.
The root-threads pop out a strong bud, lower down.

PERSEPHONE, PACKING

"I have two lives that change like dreams.
One dream, always the same,
connects the two, about to come
or able to be about to come true.
In it, I am of
my mother, or rather she
is the above-ground tree,
with me her underground and stemming
source, her feeder-rooted downtree,
whose work depends on the rock
below top-soil. If
(freezing & melting, freezing again) earth
heaves, I do not heave, but sing myself
back down warm with a story for
our sameness, our channels systemic
& open to each other's benefit.

This is just a dream
or underwater mirror
not what it would have been

if, the one facing the other,
we had ever stood still
and seen each other's face,
how gradual they are,
historical.
         As it is,
the dream goes dim with longing
to be the cause of light.
It wants to wake me up.

It can't die out or blossom;
it's stuck in autumn, impacted,
its roots spidered, replete,
like the bulb narcissus,
like daffodil & hyacinth in bulb,
or tulips, daughtering."

FESTIVAL OF BREAD

(dans l'Ain, la France profonde)

Suicide, in a village of forty heads,
is loud language—mythic but personal.
This year's been hard. A father hanged himself
in time for New Year's. Now at noon on May Day
the son's found drowned, sand in his redblond hair
face down in the shallows of a river
a fox can walk across, head above water—
a week before the hay comes in. Despair's
not a word they use. An aunt's come to stay.

The village has restored its old twelve-loaf
common oven, for a Bread Festival.
Tourists find old-time comfort in good bread.

The widow shoves her night-time self aside,
kneads silence down into dough, and lets it rise.

FULL MOON, UNSTRESSED MEASURES
(for Marilyn Hacker)

O moon, we are not Sung Chinese. We
lack the court rhythm of moon-views.
In our tradition
the moon is for metaphor
but we speak to your presence
measuring our words.

O moon we are women & travellers
whose obedience you will not
(among all earth's obedient)
have noticed. Though it is real
we are small.
We are friends,
maternal not virginal.
We stand for praise of your part
in our children.
Shine for them, far from us.
Remind them of, call them
to themselves by,
gradual intervals,
turn and return.
Regulate them lightly.

We praise your recurring,
the continuous bass of your
luminous groundwork.
We hear you. Your melodies ride
the beat of the silence between
your old light & new light.
We listen like percussionists.

In ten strokes of your pulse
a healthy woman makes a child.

Tonight you climb to your height
flamboyantly, angling
light lost to us back to us.
>   Below this terrace a gorge fills up
>   with mist you filter through,
>   until it shows you off. Olive leaves
>   break your shine into small ovals
>   which the wind stirs.
>   In the woods opposite,
>   two dogs salute you,
>   guttural, and are still.

You have been here before,
keeping faith with being
beautiful. You are used to
the attention of women your phases recall
to their generative pleasures.

To those who have walked on you, you pay
no heed. You spared them your stones,
your power untrammeled.
Your gravity orders
the meadows and mines
of the subsurface sea,
their gossip & converse,
their wave-carried rumors.

We speak plainer to each other
with you here. We can name what we fear
for our children, what discord.

At home in our street-canaled cities,
where natural beauty is human or sky,
our harbors reflect your behavior.
Our calendars mark the nights
you will signal to us.
We incorporate your cycles
arranged for two melodic lines:
short dusk/dawn, long fall/spring.
They move us to desire
the high view you hold available
above your repetitions. The lilt of it
rinses duplicity out of our ears
& lifts us. We triple the rhythm
by adding the pulse of our words,
in which the human things we shuffle
are exalted, and, exalted, ride
a tune uncramped and ample,

as natural as our light breathing
and as complex.

OCEANS

(for William Cook, drowned in Maine, and for Roy Huss,
lost in Indonesia)

Death is breath-taking. We all die young,
our lives defined by failure of the heart,
our fire drowned in failure of the lungs.
Still planning on pouring the best ripe part
of wines our need or grasp has sucked or wrung
from fruit & sun, we're stopped before we start.
Taste like talk fades from the stiffening tongue.

In reach of what we've wanted, our hope is strung
toward closing chords of accomplishment; we
grip ourselves.
                Cut off we go stunned, raw
as a land-child brought out to see only
ocean all the way to sky. Shut in awe
we wrap our secret in us as we die
unsaid, the deaf objects of good-by.

FOREIGN CORRESPONDENT

(for Margaret Fuller, drowned in shipwreck just off Fire Island, July 1850)

Margaret, always at Fire Island
I swim with you in mind,

you afraid of the sea
you ended in and as—
your neckbones chalk,
the lime of your kneecap
gone to the lobsterclaw,
and in the buoyant embrace
of saltwater, your blent chemistry.
When sandbars shift on the seafloor
they disturb your locked seachest,
its lumpy key, the victory medals
of your husband whose luck
fell just short of this shore.

Gothic at fifteen, I liked to pretend
I might find your lockbox
and dove and dove to explore
off the beach where storm-force sank you
and the bubble of your hope broke free
drowning your politics in metaphor.

I still pretend to sense you here, no ghost,
my elbows & nose out in the air of your urgency.

As the undertow makes itself felt I gulp breath
and swim harder against your destiny
riding the slipstream of your working changes
groping for the good inshore current,

my thoughts flawed but full of your prose
eager angry speculative.

A kickturn, & I check the beach-line
you likely saw flare-lit. Now
the summer waves are soft
as your lake-summer days
with Indian women, you gesturing
toward the amity common among them,
holding a baby, a shawl,
your account of this long out of print,
your histories drowned in their only versions.

I peel myself upright
out of your warm element
and walk the sand where Thoreau
all that next day went rushing
scouring the seawrack for signs,
your reticule, the sea-chest
of manuscripts, a word
from any who'd seen you.

Staring without finding, he began
to be able to think what to do,
could do nothing, gave up, and
crossed back to the mainland
over the water
glittering in windwash
transcendent with afterstorm.

AGAINST THE DARK, NEW POETS RISE

(for Christopher Baswell)

Look up, there's burning going on,
exploding old stuff into new.

It's never winter everywhere,
so the sun says. So says the sky
where, dot-to-dot, Giant Orion
hoists a winter warning
up the north of night.

Bellatrix sets out her flares
above the fires of three Magician Kings,
saying: Because we whose lives
are drawn take time burning,
summer gone is summer coming.
Look up,

look, cupped
in the blaze of the Barnard Buckle
flames of interstellar haze embrace,
sight of their nuptials given to us
by a nest, behind them,
phoenix, of generous
growing hot young stars.

WHAT THE WORN RHYMES FOUND

Wherever she looked today, she looked too late.
Everything had been a poem for years,
even the fleas, even the bread-plate,
even the anonymous funeral's tears
in face-lines they shone to illuminate.

Only the tough unsayable remains:
why she lied to them, what long lies she told,
and that is a story of such dense pain
she froze to forget it, forced it to go cold
long ago. Now & then, though, in her tested brain
the place it at last went dumb in
shows the jeweller a stain,
cyanide and gold.

CLIMBING IN BIG BEND NATIONAL PARK

This up-slope opens like Adam, and in
giant Eden the mountain's rib lies bare,
its arch gashed white, like Eve a possible
cataract spot split to its origin,
a splurge of stone curved like a pelvic floor.

Our stares falter, eye-shaped, elliptical.
We city people laugh to shrug off awe,
pupils awkward with these vast geographies.
We blink (quick curtain) then drink in what we see
with the thirst of the reach we climbed here for.

We stand above tree level. We are the trees.
We catch wind-storm breaths. Our branches claw.
We drink sky. It stretches us. We don't care.
We catch jokes & luck from thin tall blue air.

EVEN

I

Were there cliffs cupping Eden?
I think it so   just high enough
for the travel of shadows & echoes

Vegetal animal
Eden was nothing
Adam was nothing

> *Animal   vegetal*
> *he is on stage a while*
> *before he speaks*

> *From wing to wing*
> *air lifts and rustles*
> *The light is general*
> *a wonderful consonance*

Adam wakes present
in the present tense
to his present Eve

Eve comes to

Adam was nothing
not even lonely   till
Eve came to
          listening

In Eve's eyes
Adam is faced

Each is the only equal
They stand definite
the same in their luminous skins
their faces regarded the same

>   Adam is   /   Eve is
>   nothing   much yet but
>   by their same difference
>   Eden is seen to be everywhere
>   What they see is Eden
>   Being

Eve came to invent us
                invent audience
taking in hearing
she came to hear him:
                sponsa
                respondens

> *the birth of responsible life*

He would hear her
she would be there to hear

>   With trial of consonants
>   labials gutturals stops
>   out of breath
>   Adam begins: Br. Sh. Th. Kr.

The names stick.
The air waits. Eden
fades   the beasts
stop short   the river
threatens to harden.
                    Adam's skull
stammers & hurts

                                        Eve opens her ears

        She is   listening

On the waves the whorls embraced
Adam came   to her mind
as the sound of Adam

                                        Her throat aches

a great longing
"Ah," she replied

                        "ah"

        o Eve is out in the open
        a toss-up of vowels & verbs

Her diverted breath informed her

                        loosening vision & interludes
                        fluency   silence
                        a diverse civility

Aren't they something
Both are the only equal
and the speaking listener

Eden's creatures, eased, began flexing
out of their names their spines & joints
crackled & shone   acting in syntax
answering   her answering
                  flowering vines
hung fruited with stories

Through each other
microscope telescope
they look at the garden
Landscape enlarges them

The oxen lift their knees
the baboon flaunts its pink
the various frogs
touch the high pitch & low
of audible sound   Their range
arranges them   articulate

Syllables act on the two
who hearing say Syllable
—action   syntaction
how touching   what tact
Invented by listening
sound invents sentences.

The breeze drags fragrance through consensual intervals of air.

Confirmed by cliffs, their usual gaze
looked not down but across
neither upwards but on the level
at Eden   each other.
Journeys   never occurred to them
even at evening
when the only Other often arrived
and they breathed in.

> *Together they breathe*
> *that Other breath.*

                          They breathe that in & out
                          they keep on breathing.

   II

          In a sift of ash in Wales,
          at the bottom of a pit sunk
          in the crucial chamber of a passage grave,
          its stones cut & laid up dry
          5000 years ago, about, diggers found
          and anatomists identified a small
          bone of the inner ear. It is that of a girl
          8 to 10 years old, in perfect condition.

Lost is found. Salvation.
I happened to hear of it.

If I can hear this
what may I not hear

Sight's the electric hunger, though sensual Blake
says hearing's the most intimate appetite.

> Bird what do you praise Praise it
> again among the juniper plumes
> & silvered-blue juniper berrybeads

> Your birdpraise rivers the juniper air
> until I admit the incision of listening,
> and self rising easily up off the river
> evaporates altered into its liberty

III

Sundown, & under the afterglow
woods and fields fall still.
Hidden, the daycreatures drowse.
Nightcreatures step soft; rabbits go cautious
& the hunt is up for the unwary in-between.

Under the trees fireflies exclaim.
After dinner city people on vacation
hold hands, having been promised the moon
which is rising up a dark-collecting sky.
It is June, trees hold still, the breeze
holds its breath. I stroll out into the dim field
open to great horned owls, too big to fear them.

My mother & father are walking out
hand in hand in my mind of summer
into the shadowed meadow
crowded with flickering lights
in the Poconos in nineteen nineteen
under their honeymoon.

He calls them lightning bugs, she laughs & says
Fireflies though the hotel receptionist
said there were glow-worms, how funny.

They do not plan to remember it all their lives
but they do. Haunted by silence, they do.
It wasn't easily talked of. All I know is,
neither ever saw again
such shining flying in every direction,
acres of low-lying air where wild sparks
pulsed silent in the dark. Until they died,
it would flare up in them at times.

He turned the talk to the lightning of storms,
listening to her fear & attraction; always
he answered around her to keep her if he could
from hurting, with her wit where he was tender,
or with slow tears if his wit spoke.
It got better after twenty years or so.
They found themselves
each in the other's power & lost dread.
He would or she would take turns
managing to dredge up hope
in rummaging just for luck

for heaven in the marriage
that was their Lost & Found.

> Write lost as cost;
> spell fond, spell fund, spell found;
> spell band, spell bond, spell-bound.

And as well, if you will,
spell promise, premise;
> ratified,
> gratified.

IV

After judgment & the wet sacrament of slaughter,

greener than Eden, a shock of bliss to see
just past the stew & suck of reeking waters,
the earth ate sunshine under the olive trees.

Noah, his wife, their sons, their daughters
rushed to lower the gangplank. Awkward, long doubled,
unboxed & jostling, the passengers suddenly free
hustled uncoupling ashore to uncouple, suddenly free.

A NOTE ON THE TYPE

This book was set in Granjon, a computer copy of the Linotype version made by George W. Jones, who based his designs for the roman on the designs of Claude Garamond (c. 1480–1561). This Granjon more closely resembles Garamond's own work than do the various other modern types that bear his name. The *italic* of the font however *is* based on a series cut by Robert Granjon, who began his career as a type cutter in 1523 and was one of the first to practise the trade of type founder apart from that of printer.

Composition by NK Graphics, Keene, New Hampshire
Printed at The Stinehour Press, Lunenburg, Vermont
Bound at The Book Press, Brattleboro, Vermont